Lewis H Putnam

Review of the Revolutionary Elements of the Rebellion

And of the Aspect of Reconstruction

Lewis H Putnam

Review of the Revolutionary Elements of the Rebellion
And of the Aspect of Reconstruction

ISBN/EAN: 9783337187118

Printed in Europe, USA, Canada, Australia, Japan

Cover: Foto ©ninafisch / pixelio.de

More available books at **www.hansebooks.com**

THE

REVIEW

OF THE

REVOLUTIONARY ELEMENTS

OF THE REBELLION,

AND OF THE

ASPECT OF RECONSTRUCTION;

WITH A PLAN TO RESTORE HARMONY BETWEEN THE TWO RACES
IN THE SOUTHERN STATES.

BY A COLORED MAN.

BROOKLYN, L. I.

OCTOBER 1868.

To the People of the United States.

The design of the Review, as indicated by its title, is to note with care the new birth of the Republic and to bring the colored people into the foreground where they may be seen as the advocates of the union between the two races, and upon the basis that will secure freedom and elevation on one hand and peace and good-will on the other.

But while it may be right that the colored people should stand back until the position for them is established through the genius and the magnanimity of the dominant race, yet the sublimity of the work, to build up the Republic with the new materials at hand, and the necessity of testing their skill and usefulness in the new field where *the destiny of the nation* has placed them, will fully justify the attempt to create such ideas in the history of the times as will make a profound impression in their favor in the minds of the American people. As the time has arrived to redeem the "solemn pledge" of fidelity made to the friends who first led the author into the mission, and the fact that the purpose of the declaration as written contained the principles which aimed at the elevation of the colored people of the United States, it will be sufficient to strip it of all assumption and at the same time show the grandeur of the subject, and the overwhelming effect that will follow from the development of the plan for the accomplishment of that object. Viewing it at that time as the initiative to the reformation in the institutions that were organized for the management of the philanthropy of the nation, and make the result redound to the glory of the American people by the elevation of the proscribed race of the country, it will present a feature sufficiently grand to command the approbation it will aim to secure by the publication of this work.

If the philanthropists and the statesmen were guided by the spirit of justice in the attempts to represent the colored man at any time in the history of the country previous to the war, or if they had a clear conception of the requirements of the nation, there would have been no necessity for the efforts made by me to overturn the policy by which they were governed until the solution of the several questions were reached by the Rebellion. But the fact that through their apathy or want of appreciation, the people of the United States lost the opportunity to realize the benefit of the plan written by the colored man to shield the country from civil war, and the fact that its existence was known to a leading member in the Cabinet and to others in Congress, and was resorted to at the eleventh hour to conciliate the border States, will make it an important feature in the efforts to establish the position for the reprerosentative men of my race.

In rising to the surface from the depth where the author was buried by those who were struggling to occupy the position they were unqualified to fill, the first duty is to proclaim the solemn fact that the time has come to assume the duty and secure a general recognition of the mission in the name of his race and country. It will be sustained by the magnitude of the work that has been accomplished for that purpose, and to make up a record sufficiently brilliant to maintain the integrity of the projector of the revolution that was designed to sweep out of existence the powerful but useless benevolent institutions that stood in the way to control the sympathy of the public in behalf of the colored people, without conferring upon them any corresponding benefit. While the ulterior object of this grand movement was hid from the public, yet it was fully known to the leading managers, who made the most decided efforts to shield themselves from the consequences of its development, but as they have lost the power to command the situation, it is important that the result should be announced as the first victory of the pen of the colored man over the genius of the dominant class!

It was the basis of the plan for the extinction of the "peculiar institution of the Southern States," as it will be seen by the exposition of the secret history of the efforts to inspire prominent men of the two sections of the country with the spirit adequate for the accomplishment of the work with the agency of Congress, and thereby save it from the terrible civil war it has undergone. But in spite of their brilliant intellect in other things, yet, in this field of labor they were not only powerless in the attempt to stay it, but there are contingencies that must be provided for with other remedies than those indicated in any of the plans for the restoration of the Union. "As one born in due season" to labor in the name of the colored people without exciting the sensibility of the dominant race, it is necessary that the claims upon the attention of all should be established free from any party proclivity, and without concealing the ulterior purpose. To this end, the plan will be submitted with the details indicating its ramifications, and with the proof of the inflexible integrity with which the mission has been sustained it will carry with it sufficient weight to justify the dedication of this work to the people of the United States by

Their obedient servant,

L. H. PUTNAM.

BROOKLYN, L. I., *April* 13, 1868.

CHAP. I.

THE REVOLUTIONARY ELEMENTS OF THE REBELLION CAREFULLY CONSIDERED.

As nothing can be submitted to the country, that ought to command a greater degree of attention than the complications that have followed the measures for the adjustment and for the restoration of the union, it is important that the subject should be carefully considered from the necessities of the general knowledge and the harmony that should prevail in the minds of the people of the two sections. For while the work for the political regeneration of the Southern States has been carried forward with the greatest vigor, yet, the elements that underlie the strata of reconstruction must either be considered at this juncture, or be met at a disadvantage, when the means to deal with them will be out of existence.

The first supposition is, that the work upon the battle field having been accomplished, that the spirit that led to the commencement of the strife is paralyzed ,leaving the people in no other condition than that of submission ? If the means to ascertain the fact as to how far the feelings of the secessionists have been trained into loyalty by the bayonet of the Union soldier, and that the acceptance of the situation will be realized in the stability of civil government ushered into existence under the new order of things; then, indeed, the time is at hand when fraternity and industry will consolidate the interests of the two races into a common union under the Federal Government. But this is the bright side, with nothing to sustain the hopes that reconstruction will be successfully carried out without infusing into the resources of the Southern States the vitality contemplated by the people under the teaching of their leading men and by whom they were driven into the rebellion.

The chief stone of the corner of the Confederate Government was Slavery; and the edifice erected upon it, adorned as it was with all the glittering hopes of the builders, now lies buried beneath the ruins ! The grand idea now is, to aid in hewing out another through the genius of freemen and place it under the Federal Government, that its strength may be increased to the extent necessary to support freedom in the entire country with the concurrence of the people.

The force by which the first link of the chain of the Union was broken by secession, and by which the power of the general government was destroyed for the time, is a subject that cannot be lost sight of without committing a fatal mistake, when it is considered that the feelings of the people were fired with a degree of hostility that may still excite them to the extent that their opposition may paralyze the power of the civil authority. How to deal with them, is the question that every colored man must feel with sufficient weight to justify the attention the subject will demand from the standpoint it will be considered in their behalf. For while universal emancipation has come upon the country "from its military necessity," and has opened the avenues to all the rights and immunities necessary for the elevation of the freemen, yet, to incorporate these principles in the organic laws and effectually change the autonomy of the non-reconstructed States by virtue of the power of the Federal Government, is the result that could only *follow from the guidance of an unseen hand.* This is the political avalanche that has buried the traditional policy of one section, and it will recoil upon the other and create a common level for every State of the Union. But whatever may be the policy of the Loyal States in reference to the equalization of the suffrage as a national measure, yet everything that is sacred to freedom and would promote the prosperity of the country, demands that there should be but one destiny and that it should be fixed by the united efforts of the people.

The breaking up of the relations between the two races, resulting in the general disorganization of society, without any landmarks to guide to harmony ; and superinduced as it may have been by causes over which the country had no control, yet it is a revolution in the Republic that all good men must deplore, in spite of the regenerating features it has brought with it. And why ? because the rancor that has been engendered and the humiliation inflicted upon the people upon whom the weight of the calamity has fallen, will require the most earnest labor of the statesman to obliterate it.

For the Appomattox surrender was in itself more than an ordinary incident in the fortune of war from the political consequences it involved, and yet, in point of importance it will weigh next to nothing in comparison with the disaster that has overwhelmed the people by the extinction of the dogma of secession, and in the elevation of the freedmen as the counterpoise to the principles that governed the statesmen of Secessia. If they had gone into that great *struggle with the aid of the colored man and with the emblem of Freedom emblazoned upon the banners that waved upon the battle-fields, the impression is, that his support would have led to a revision of the map of the United States.* If, then, the fatal results attending the want of affinity between the leaders in the rebellion and the emancipation of the colored people, is fully established in the minds of all intelligent men, then nothing can be fixed with more clearness than the landmarks that will warn the country of the dangers that would attend any reactionary measures against equal liberty in the Southern States.

CHAP. II.

The Last Hours of the Confederate Congress and the Question of Emancipation.

The key note which was sounded in the last hours of the sitting of the Confederate Congress, when the question of emancipation and the enrolment of colored men as soldiers to fight their battles, was submitted for consideration by the statesmen who saw in that measure their only salvation, must be taken as the true guide, and will enable them to point out the future policy of the country with an unerring hand.

It is universally admitted that the "Institution," which led to the war for its preservation, was the source of weakness that was fatal to the Confederate Government, and paved the way for the humiliation that followed the terrible catastrophe as the sequel of the rebellion. If the people can study anything from it, they will learn that the first requirement of free government in the Southern States is the extinction of caste, and is the sentiment that should be diffused in that section of the country to enable them to work with the earnestness by which they may rise again and lead in the revolution inaugurated by the emancipation of the colored people, and which underlies the measures for the reconstruction of the Republic. While it is true that the work of freedom and elevation did not originate with the Southern people, yet it is equally true that it should have, and hence the necessity of a clear conception of the situation which must be seized upon by them as the basis to establish the union between the two races.

The fact that the military bill is insufficient in itself for the accomplishment of the work, inasmuch as an important part will fall upon those who are ostracised by that measure, will be fully realized when it is considered that to secure a freehold interest in the soil for the freedmen will depend upon the concessions that may be made for that purpose by the planters, and without any reference to their loyalty.

The *Revolutionary Elements of the Rebellion which have fixed the destiny of the Southern States, take their source from the measures adopted by the nation for the preservation of the Republic, and may be classified with the exploits upon the battle fields, where liberals and conservatives stood side by side under the guidance of the power created by the constitution, and called into requisition by exigencies that were wholly unprovided for by the framers of that instrument.* To consummate the work with the sword without the agency of the national council was an *impossibility, and yet, to reconcile the people to the means employod for that purpose, is the task which stands in its magnitude equal to the efforts for the suppression of the rebellion.*

But to look upon the destructive ideas that may exist in the opposition to the enfranchisement of the colored people, is the duty that must be considered in connection with the fact that all the Northern planks used in the construction of the platforms to sustain the "peculiar institution" of the Southern States, were split up and broken into fragments by its weight and every thing lost to the cause they were designed to support.

The next phase it presents in the regular order of things, is the Civil Governments inaugurated by national legislation, which gives the subject a novel aspect, and has infused into it a vitality far greater than it could ever attain by any other means, and the question is, will the acceptance of the situation by the people make it the initiative to the measures for their relief, from the humiliation that followed the downfall of the Confederate States, and reconcile them to the enfranchisement of the freedmen? Was it a measure forced upon the nation by the disorganized condition of things, which made it the only safeguard against anarchy, and enables it to stand in the position to calm the minds of the people by its patriotic mediation? In the answer to this question, let the voice of the colored people be heard!

While nothing could be more grand and providential in its conception than reconstruction upon the basis of equal liberty for all, and while it will open the only field to reach the most elevated position in the work to restore the freedmen to the soil as the agricultural class, and thereby give emancipation its true value, yet nothing but the irresistable decree by which it was forced upon the country, has led to its acceptance, and enables the friends of freedom to proclaim in the language of the Declaration of Independence *that all men are free and equal.*

Proclaim it far and near, that it is the result of the revolution created by the rebellion that is sweeping out of existence the pro-slavery elements by which the nation was governed from its foundation, and that it is the great source of relief for the statesmen whose genius was tarnished by the degrading labor imposed upon them to delude the masses with the false impression that the dogma which underlies republican institutions in this country that all are free and equal, means politically the white man. It was by the teaching of this heresy that the veneration for the constitution of the United States was lost with the patriotism that gave it its existence and reduced that instrument to the standard of the Delphic enigma, making it the source of confusion in the minds of the people. Therefor let all good men repudiate the chimerical ideas which contaminate the mind, and let Democracy in its purity rule the nation through the wisdom and unceasing vigilancy of the people concentrated in the National Congress, where the divine attribute, as manifested by the extension of equal suffrage to all, will be maintained and radiate to every part of the great commonwealth through the Legislatures of the several States.

The precipitancy with which universal freedom in its reality was launched upon the country by the surrender at Winchester, and paralyzed the minds of those who were wholly unprepared for the duty it imposed upon the loyal and patriotic masses to accept with sincere serenity the ideas of *equality* and *fraternity*, yet, it is the pre-requisite to the recognition of that class of American citizens who were elevated to the exalted position by the power of a higher law than that of man. But to suppose that that sublime principle will become universal with the agency of the bayonet or by the amendment of the Federal constitution, is to hope against hope, as long as a large portion of the people are only convinced against their will.

The counterpoise to all reäctionary measures is in the mission of the colored man, who has been brought upon the political surface and stands erect in the position where he was placed by the destiny of the nation, and to approach the contending parties, made up with the lóyal and patriotic liberal and conservative minds in one section in connection with the Union men, and the secessionists of the Southern States, to take counsel for the adjustment of the differences that neutralize the efforts to promote the fraternal relations that make up the unity of the republic, is the first and the most important duty that will be performed in their behalf by Congress.

The first point submitted in behalf of the race, is, that as the constitution of the United States was no barrier to the commencement of the civil war, and that its force was paralyzed by the belligerent measures employed for that purpose on one side, and as the existence of the republic on the other was only sustained by the loyalty of the government and the people under the law of self-preservation, therefore, no adjustment is possible under its provisions which makes it necessary that all should agree to establish the basis of the reünion by the acceptance of the situation as indicated and accepted by the conventions and the legislatures of the several States.

The second point is, that emancipation and the enfranchisement of the citizens by virtue of the military plan ot reconstruction as a national measure should be recognized and the principles embodied in the organic laws of every State in either section of the country, to maintain the consistency and the dignity of the nation, and inspire the people of the Southern States with the necessary energy to work fully up to the requirements of the new condition of things.

CHAP. III.

THE NATIONAL ASPECT OF RECONSTRUCTION.

The critical view of the subject in its national aspect at this juncture, may afford the means to see how far the loyal States will go into the measures imposed upon the country. For, as nothing could be more serious in its tendency to undermine the Republic than the repudiation of the suffrage bill adopted by Congress, in the face of the fact that its force must be the same in every State, it is of the highest importance that the attempt should be made to draw the attention of the people to it, as they must see the justice of the demand it will impose. The necessity for the legislation by which the inherent rights of State legislatures and conventions to control the suffrage, were surrendered to meet the exigincies of the nation by the adoption of the military bill, will sink far deeper into the vitals of the Republic than the mind can penetrate through the confusion the subject presents at this juncture. The sacrifices the people are called upon to make by the prompting of their patriotism to·preserve the government of the country, by the efforts to purify the organic Laws of every Loyal State of the proscriptive provisions which stands as the barrier to the political elevation of the colored man, not merely as an act of justice 'to him, but to increase the sublimity of the work of their Representatives to fix the destiny of the Southern States. For it cannot be supposed by any thinking mind, that the validity of the measures of enfranchisement, will only apply to one section and not to the other, for that would constitute a discrimination wholly incompatible with the rights of these commonwealths, when the position in which these States will stand in the Union, is considered. This has come upon the country by the centralization of power in the Federal Government that was exercised previous to the war by the States, that constitutes the revolution, and its magnitude will only be seen by the proceedings of the people in the Conventions and the Legislatures where the suffrage question as a national measure must be considered. The first phase in the advance to centralization, is in the consolidated efforts to crush the rebellion with the sword, and as that catastrophe is the result of the work of all who filled their position in the ranks of the Union armies, or contributed material or moral means for their support upon the battle field, therefore, for weal or wo it must redound to the nation. From that point, none who have survived the great contest can recede or pause to exhibit any sympathy for the Southern people, that could not be extended to them in the hour of need without the betrayal of a degree of weakness that is neither useful nor dignified. In the dispersal of the Confederate armies, the people were again made subjects of the Government of the United States, but to what extent they are loyal, is the grave question, and on its solution the stability of the Republic will depend. Driven as they were, from every position of any political importance, and thrown back upon their own vigor, and upon the internal resources of the seceded States, they cannot fail to learn the true value of the only allies among them that will serve the purpose for their elevation. For they have tried the strength of the planks of the platforms upon which their hopes were concentrated, and the fact, that the fragments lie scattered in every direction, while the power they had in others, is lost, will warn the South of the delusion of the future.

Let it be proclaimed from every house-top, and be re-echoed through the valleys of the country, that the true friends of the Southern States will labor for the equalization of the principles imposed upon them by the incorporation of the same in the organic laws of every State of the Union. Let it be proclaimed again and again, that the most sacred and solemn task that makes up the political existence of the several States have been performed in the conventions by the white man and the colored man for the first time in the history of the nation, in compliance with the will of the people as expressed by their Representatives in Congress, and that the grand spectacle shall make up the new era in the Government of the United States. Force upon the country the consideration of the fact that political equality and fraternity to exist in one section of the country, will destroy all the opposition to it in the others.

The supposition that the colored man was born for servitude and to labor in the cotton field exploded on the field of battle in the great struggle with the rebellion, where the proof was exhibited that bravery is a natural instinct in him as it is in the Caucasian race. Hid as it was by oppression for 240 years in this country, yet, with the light of liberty to guide him through the darkness created by prejudice against the race, they will move forward with all the vigor with which they are inspired by patriotism. *Sneer who may at any deformity, whether of the heel, nose, the lips, head or hair of the colored people, yet it will fail to extinguish the fact that they are framed as they were intended to be by the God of Nature, and that they are bound by all that is sacred in Heaven to stand up in its defence or gloriously fall in the effort to do their duty as Freemen at any cost.* If the betrayal of freedom will be the downfall of the Republic, let those who would restrict the suffrage by any discrimination that would extend to one race and not to the others, take heed. The true value of this right lies in its use as the extinguisher of discontent in the minds of the people, and makes it the safeguard of free institutions. While the colored people in the Northern States, who form nothing more than mere cyphers in the political world, the time is at hand when the Empire State, with Pennsylvania and Ohio, will be equal with Massachusetts in the elevation of their sable citizens to positions of honor and trust. For the danger that underlies this subject will be seen in the tendency to consolidate freedom in the Southern States, where their hopes will be fully concentrated under leaders who will be governed by circumstances without any reference to any sympathy for the Union. For in spite of the inflexible loyalty of any people, the irresistible power of wealth and education must be considered as the controlling elements in the government of the State and its destiny.

CHAP. IV.

The Power of the Federal Government over the several States.

As the amendment to the constitution of the United States, and the civil rights bill adopted by Congress, have made the government the custodian of freedom, it is important to take a view of the means that may be employed to enable it to fulfil the mission. If it was possible to bring out a decision from the Supreme Court to

settle the question in reference to the duty of the States that are
not under the operation of the military bill, that would force them
to be governed by its spirit the same, and that a ready compliance
would be accorded by Maryland, Kentucky and Missouri; then the
work of regeneration would, in effect, be accomplished, and would
serve as a shield against the exigency that would require means
more weighty to carry it out. The extinction of State Sovereignty,
where it conflicts with the power of the Federal Government,
seems to be an accomplished fact, or at any rate the scope of the
power it has attained is sufficient to secure compliance in every
case where the general interests of the country may require
it. But to resort to harsh measures, would be so clearly
incompatible with the existence of the civil government of the
States, that it is worth while to examine with care the remedy at
hand. The first object is, to fix upon a clear and comprehensive
line of policy to protect the people without infringing upon their
rights, and yet this will depend upon the vigor of the Legislatures
in the reörganization of the judiciary and the militia of the State
upon the basis that must be sufficiently firm and complete to preclude the necessity for any extra aid from Congress or the military
of the departments. The stern reality that exists in the predomi-
nant portion of the population in many of the localities in every
one of the non-reconstructed States, is made up of that class that were
suddenly transformed into manhood, and is well calculated to perplex
and paralyze the judgment of those who have either controlled or
regarded them with such a degree of indifference as to lead to the
impression that this people have no rights that white men are
bound to respect. To recognize and surrender to the new element
in the body politic from the necessity of the case, is the true test of
the loyalty upon which the strength of the country will depend.
The rapid advance that has been made up to this line of duty by
eminent men of the two sections, is the most sublime aspect that
the new order of things could present, and to cherish the principles
by which they are governed is essential to the success of the work
that must be performed to overcome all antagonism that would
impede the union between the two people.

But to overcome the difficulties that stand in the way of the
measures necessary to create a regular system for the operation of the
judiciary and for the administration of equal and exact justice to all,

is no ordinary task, for it is the success of that object that will relieve the military of the duty imposed upon it by the present disordered condition of things. It is this stream that flows through all civilized communities, and takes its source from Divine teaching for the control of the moral government of man; and its pollution from whatever cause will lead to anarchy and demoralization. No class of people could ever be exposed to greater danger from it than the freedmen, who may become the victims of imposition with no other dependence than the court of justice which may be to them a source of injustice for years to come, from those who may have no sympathy with Freedom. For whether situated in the immediate neighborhood of large communities, or in the remote localities in the agricultural districts, justice is due to all, from the highest to the humblest. To secure this blessing, it is within the power of the National Government to infuse its spirit into the Legislatures, and to watch over the people until the judicial system shall attain the vigor that will make it equal to the duty that lies before it. To organize the militia of the several States and bring it up to the perfection that will make it equal to any emergency, is the most serious part of the work, and will be fully appreciated by the South and the Federal Government. Any reluctance to approach it will only indicate the want of information in reference to the vital principles the nation must inculcate in the public mind by the prompting of the laws of self-preservation. The attempt to shun this duty will not avail or relieve it from the responsibility it has assumed in instituting free Government, which points to the future when the battalions of infantry, the squadrons of cavalry and the batteries of artillery will exist and be governed by the same rules and regulations for all, and with no special privilege for any. The stern necessity that demands it can only be understood by keeping in view the fact that all proscription by the action of the Federal Government will be at an end. The right to the spur was won during the rebellion, but not awarded to any of those who were considered worthy of it by some of the disciples of West Point and others high in rank in the army. But the true policy of the nation will be fully developed in carrying out the plan for the organization of the national guard, and will test the spirit that controls its efforts to break down caste in the United States. It will present the grandest spectacle of the time when the million of sable sentinels of

Freedom will watch over the Goddess of Liberty and at the same time aid in maintaining the peace of the country by their neutrality. It is to carry this, the last entrenchment of the prejudice of the country, that the rally will be made to secure the triumph that will constitute them the custodians of Freedom, therefore, let the purpose be proclaimed far and near, that the exercise of this right by all freemen will be the finality of the struggle to break down the barrier to their elevation.

CHAP. V.

THE DUTY OF THE FREEDMEN IN THE SOUTHERN STATES. · .

While it is proper and right that all the privileges belonging to the colored people should be presented to the country in the strongest light, and in every phase of the transition in which they must be seen, yet, there is an important duty connected with the subject that should be considered with a view to make some reference to the paramount object that lies before them in the relations they are called upon to sustain to the community at large. The sudden transformation, effecting the social condition of four millions of people, and the chaos resulting from the breaking up of their relations with the soil, is sufficiently grave to justify the attention that will be devoted to it under the caption selected for that purpose. There would be less cause for apprehension at this time, if the people were actuated by the disposition to follow the demands of justice in reference to the destiny of the colored people in this country, but the fact that the nation is governed by the force of circumstances in all things that make up its policy on the subject of Freedom, cannot but create the impression that they may stop short of the line of duty to their posterity.

The first part of the work before the colored man, is to make such an impression upon the minds of the American people as will create the weight he will employ to control the sentiments of the public. The half and half measures by which the nation entered into the design to settle the suffrage question, was paralyzed by rejecting the constitutional amendment by the States it was intended to affect, and which, if adopted, could not but extinguish the only ray of light in the political horizon of the colored people. It was an attempt to abandon coercion and impose it upon the people to legislate the principle into existence for the relief of the nation from the most important duty that could devolve upon it by the demands of freedom and self-protection. Its acceptance by the legislatures of the Loyal States made up for the time the policy they were ready to adopt and extinguish the spark of liberty, but it was rekindled by those who were opposed to emancipation, and to the military necessity that gave it an existence.

The principles that were concealed under the assumed magnanimity, were not only void of any national dignity from the want of ingenuousness, but it was only useful as a measure for self-stultification by its adoption.

It was the impression that the Civil Rights bill aimed at the elevation of the citizens of all the States to the level where they would be recognized as the custodians of freedom, under the government of the United States, and with the co-operation of the legislatures of the several States. This must either be the result of reconstruction, or the germ of future commotion between the two sections of the country. To make a clear discrimination between the duty that rightfully belongs to the several States, and the relations of the masses to the Union, is a delicate task, and yet it must be performed with a view to fix their allegiance without any dependence upon mere party machinery for its existence, for whatever may be the danger of internal war, it will only come from this source, although there need be no apprehension if the power necessary for the regulation of civil government could be judiciously directed with the concurrent efforts of influential minds of all shades of opinion. It would afford a far better field for the developement of public sentiment, which, if concealed at this juncture, may show itself in the future, with a degree of violence that may be strong enough to neutralize the entire work of reconstruction, for, if it was possible to punish any portion of the people for treason against the United States, those who would be the subjects of judicial proceedings should be known, and all others should or may be exempt from the disabilities. But under the present plan of proceedure there seems to be chances for committing very grave mistakes by the exercise of discretionary power by subordinate officials, who may be very honest in their intentions, and yet, from mere presumption, they may proscribe and inflict punishment, by the adoption of measures that should only be the result of the decision of a regular tribunal. But while the oath of allegience to the Government may be an important relief to those who may comply with its requirements, it will not shield those who may refrain from availing themselves of its benefits, from any scruples they may have as ex-secessionists. But is it right to put in any plea for them as citizens of the United States, that it may be seen how far all loyal men may respect them in their situation? It is to make some use of this class why a regular system to'organize civil government should be adopted to infuse the same degree of vitality into the minds of the people in each of the unreconstructed States, as will enable them to move on in the direct line of action in the conventions and legislatures, as will be similar in every case where the purpose is to consolidate and build up such principles for the commonwealth as will preclude the antagonism that would otherwise exist, by excluding one class of citizens from the enjoyment of privileges that were exercised by the other.

The position of the colored people as supporters of the work of reconstruction, seems to be mixed up with so many extraneous ideas that the efforts to define and give them a direction that will be more comprehensive, is essential and paramount as their success will depend upon it; for however useful they may have been to the Union cause during the rebellion, and the fact that the spirit of the principles that they are called upon to support at the ballot box, takes its source from the same necessity, and yet the social status of this people is the same in either section of the country. From this standpoint the question must occur, that the answer may show how far the people will be prepared to realize the danger that would result from the attempt to use the colored man as a mere straw upon the political surface for the benefit of the Union, at the expense of his interest in the Southern States.

Will this nation take heed from the fatal mistake committed by the sacrifice of the great dogma that was proclaimed to the world in 1776, that "all men are born free and equal," while the convention of 1787 recognized property in man and made it the germ of the rebellion? The want of a holy purpose in the policy of the Government of the United States on the subject of Equal Liberty for all, seems to be very seriously felt in all its measures, and if the disposition to shun the responsibility of the crisis should be manifested as it was in the adjustment at that time, it will be impossible to maintain the peace of the Republic.

The introduction of the necessary measures for the guidance of the colored people in the midst of the transition and the vigor with which the developments will be made, will be sufficient to give all the animation they may require to enable them to make the impression that with them freedom is sacred. To date the rights of these people as citizens of this country from the issuing of the proclamation of emancipation, would be simply a subterfuge and an indignity, and would indicate the deceptive intent of those who are only half-way men, and who will stop short in the midst of the work, at the first moment that will serve as the opportunity. The fact that there should be no cause for any hostility between the two people in the Southern States, ought to be clearly seen, and every measure resorted to to devise the means to subdue the prejudices by which they are separated from each other. To accomplish this vital object, all the sacrifices that can be made without debasing the dignity of the man, or endangering the holy cause, must be resorted to for that purpose. The view of the grand flank movement upon the entire line of the opponents of Freedom from the point contemplated, will not only be highly important to the colored people, but the salvation of the Southern States will depend upon its success. It will give a degree of force to the energies of that section of the country, far greater than it has ever had, and create the means for self-dependence to the extent that will be fully sustained by the development of its resources. Mixed up as this irresistible purpose is with the existence of those who now lie postrate by the power that extinguished the rebellion, they cannot but see in it the means of the deliverance they must seek in the alliance of the people of the South. Therefore, to. drive out the Freedmen is an impossibility, for they were planted among the people by the laws that gave the power to the peculiar institution, and by their natural rights, and owing allegiance to no other country they are citizens of the United States, and any hostile design carried into operation against them, could not fail to recoil upon the nation.

The several congresses held by the people of the Southern States, from time to time, some years before they seceded, it is known that the labor question was the most perplexing to their public men, and whatever power they may possess to carry on the industry of the country in the future, the very first and the main object will be to secure the aid of the Freedmen as a class that they never will supplant. It is not only necessary to shield them from the life and death struggle that would follow from any attempt to drive them out, but it is necessary for the preservation of the Republic. The means by which the solution of the grand problem will be reached to indicate the fraternal relations of the people to each other, will be clearly manifested by touching the leading points of the plan of reconstruction.

The importance of a definite conception of the work as it is, should be understood by colored men to enable them to perform their duty to the country with all the intelligence necessary to show the spirit with which they will be governed as supporters of the Union, and it can not be too carefully considered, for they must have a position strong enough to guard against any invasion of their rights. For whatever may be the views of others in reference to reconstruction, with the colored people their plan must be fixed in the supervision of the nation which would not only be extended to the adoption of the constitution by the several States and the organization of the Legislatures, but it will include civil Government and the establishing of an effective police system, and the organization and the equipment of the militia free from all proscription, and thereby put every branch in a complete working order before the surrender to the people of the power assumed during the war in behalf of the Republic. It will be the only effective protection against mere paper concessions in behalf of Freedom, and will neutralize the facilities to cheat at the ballot box and paralyze the entire labor of the statesmen with the sacrifices made upon the field of battle, as would be the case as soon as those who are now in the back ground shall have come to the front.

It is to guard against the provocation that would excite them to any re-actionary measure, either against Freedom or the Policy of the Government, why the suggestion is made to commit them to the work of reconstruction, which, if carried out under its guidance, and in accordance with the principles that may be embodied in a general plan to be followed by the conventions and the legislatures of the several States, it could not be regarded as the triumph of one party over the other, which in either case, may carry with it a proscription that would be felt by the minority with a degree of keenness that would necessarily engender antagonism. The object is to extinguish the fire of Secession, and to reconstruct society with the new materials, with a view to its permanency by the removal of the volcanic elements that underlie the strata of the work of the politician who labors with no ambition to reach the elevation of the statesman. Therefore, it is not the special duty of the colored man to study the difference and learn something of the seriousness of the danger that should be avoided if possible, but it is for the entire people of this country, who will control its destiny at the ballot box, that must go into it with a clearness of conception far greater than they have evinced up to the present time.

Those who are in favor of peace, let them show their plan and the method by which they will work to promote it. For the public men who have no other stock in trade than the force of the opposition they can array against each other, by exciting the feelings of the masses without having any principles to inculcate to advance the general interest of the State or the Nation, will never make anything else of themselves but mere agitators. It is the category that every intelligent colored man should avoid, and if they would be useful to this generation, let them study the means, and learn the true value of political economy as a science, that they may labor with credit to the race and for the good of the country. But while it is the duty of all good Citizens to cultivate the means to live in peace with each other, and only learn the art of war for the protection of Freedom or the defence of the country, yet in case of any attack on either from any scource, let it be the religious duty of every colored man to fill his place in the rank of his regiment, and be ready to move forward at the command and strike with all the vigor that God and nature may supply to carry on the sacred work.

CHAP. VI.

THE PLAN TO RESTORE HARMONY BETWEEN THE TWO RACES IN THE
SOUTHERN STATES, AND FOR SOCIAL IMPROVEMENT ON THE BASIS
OF AGRICULTURE.

The future of the United States, or of the Southern States, will
present no subject that will be more important to the happiness of
the people, than the science of agriculture, whether considered as
the field for speculation, or for the elevation of the race that stood
before the nation as the hewers of wood and the drawers of water.
Its grandeur will be seen in the fact that the polluted stream of
politics will be subordinate to it in every phase, which enable them
to realize the power it will exert to control the efforts to consolidate
freedom, and restore the relations of the freedmen to the soil as the
agricultural class. The antagonism that has taken such a wide
range between capital and labor in this country, requires a solution
that will lead to a reciprocity of interests, that will be more permanent, at the same time have the inherent means to regulate itself
without being exposed to the discordancy that effects, to a greater
or less degree, the great interests of the manufactories of the New
England States and elsewhere; for, notwithstanding the redun-
dant population which makes up the masses in all the cities,
and the constant flow of the tide of emigration from Europe, yet
the struggle continues under the various organizations to the detri-
ment of the mutual relations that should be sustained between
the employers and the employees.

But in turning to the Southern States, where the principle of
the social revolution will prevail, it is necessary to examine the
field that the future of the two races will present not only to the
people of the United States; but with the view to make it equally
as useful to the Brazilian Empire, as to the colonies of Spain, where
the transition from slavery to freedom will follow the light kindled
in this country. For whatever may be said or written in reference to the regulation of labor, by the law of supply and demand, in the sense in which it may be considered in large communities, and in the agricultural regions in the Eastern, Northern
or Western States, yet nothing would be more useless to the freedmen than the theory of the philosophers of the day, who, with their

ancient ideas, which leads them to the conclusion that these people will be safe as tenants-at-will, and that you must "let them alone to root or die." But while there can be no doubt but what a large portion of the freedmen will, by their industry, become free-holders under the usual process of the law of trade, nevertheless, as the relations between them and the soil were broken up by the sovereignty incidental in the government of the United States, and exercised to meet the great contingency of the war, it is important that it should in some way guard against the disorder that would follow from the surrender to the respective States of the charge it assumed for their protection; for it is not the freedmen alone that requires the protection, but it is a society, made up as it is of the incongruities, which is the result of the education which carries with it no power of cohesion.

To leave the people in such a situation to depend upon what may be called the drifting policy, to restore every thing to their normal condition as indicated by the class of men who have nothing to suggest, would be a calamity equal in its tendency to the defeats they suffered upon the battle field, inasmuch as it would leave them to struggle with the chaotic elements of the war, that were created to a very great extent by the operations carried on in behalf of the United States. To teach all classes of the people how to live for the mutual benefit of society under the present condition of things, is a necessity that will not admit of any delay by those who feel the force of the exigency to the extent that will urge them on in the efforts to comply with its demands as benefactors of that portion of this country that has experienced to a limited degree the benign influence of civilization, or the blessings of Republican Institutions. In this connection, the demoralization of the financial resources of the country must be considered, to ascertain the extent of the necessity for national aid to the people, to enable them to recuperate from the prostration under which they are suffering, without making any sacrifices of their lands, and thereby give the speculators the advantages that should only be enjoyed by those who may enter into the spirit of the design to make agriculture the basis of elevation in the Southern States.

The despondency in the minds of some of the people at this juncture, may afford rare opportunities to the modern Shylocks to purchase lands from those who in too many instances, will be ready to eat up all that they may have, and shut themselves out for all time to come from the high position they could occupy among the planters under the new system of support to agricultural developments. But as useful as private capital may be to the commercial world, yet it would be wholly inadequate to meet the demands necessary to give a vitality to agricultural interest equal to the requirements of that great branch of industry. From this view of the subject, the question that must recur and press itself upon the attention of the political economists, is, will it be the duty of the nation to advance as a loan the sum of $50,000,000, to be increased to $100,000,000 if necessary, for the relief of the planters in the non-reconstructed States, upon the condition herein stated? The $40,000,000 of the surplus revenue deposited with the several States some years since, was thrown away in *comparison with the great results that would follow from the application of the proposed loan, by which the people of the Southern States could be placed in the position to realize the leading objects contemplated by the Statesmen in their reflections upon the felicity under the* Empire *they aimed to establish in that section.*

The *l'amour propre* that may develop itself from the first impression that may be created in the minds of those who may be struggling with their early convictions, would to some extent paralyze the principles that underlie the plan for national aid, but the fact that there must be some means to overcome sectional prejudices, and fire the fraternal feelings of the people of the two sections of the country and from the force of its application sway their judgment in the right direction. The thirty years' training that was necessary to bring them up to the labor they have undergone during the last six years will become obsolete from the rapidity with which they will advance in the new ideas which leads to peace and prosperity, instead of strife and rapine. The people will learn something from the sacrifices made by the South when considered in the light in which they can be seen and will show that all the materials to establish Freedom in this country were furnished from that section, and at the cost of more than $1,200,000,000 of dollars and add to this sum $3,000,000,000 lost by investments made in Confederate Bonds and $4,200,000,000 by the depositors of greenbacks issued during the war, and the aggregate will be fully equal to the expenditure of the Government of the United States. What will they receive in return for the vast outlay, except from the increase in the value of the lands ? The answer to this question lies far deeper than can be imagined by many of the statesmen who only see everything from the surface. But, view it as you may, it is the Pandora box of Secession, and if it should be opened, the agitation for compensation would be the first fruit of the poison'that it would emit.

But as the connecting link between the two races must depend upon the agricultural developments as the life of the industry of the future, it demands an elaborate exposition to illuminate as far as possible the minds of those who are satisfied to follow the condition of things under which the colored people have struggled since emancipation in the State of New York and elsewhere in the Northern States. For while the impression exists in the public mind, that they must necessarily enjoy all the rights of labor in common with the dominant class in this section of the country, yet, in view of the fact that the combination against them is carried to the extent where nothing is seen of them as mechanics, it ought to be sufficient to dispel the delusion that must be overcome to open the way for the acceptance of the principles that will be submitted to the nation in their behalf. If from that cause and their rigid exclusion from all the avenues of general industry as opened to others, the degradation of this people can be clearly traced, then the case will be made up in accordance with the facts, which shows, that notwithstanding the sympathy and the liberality extended to them in connection with their equality before the law, their condition is not far removed from that of servitude !

With all the gratitude that should be manifested by them for the sympathy of those who are opposed to oppression, yet the colored people must have something more substantial to stand upon than what they have realized from freedom in the State of New York or elsewhere in any of the free States, where they are the victims of an intolerable proscription as a powerless minority. Trained up as they are in the school of experience, with no affinity to the community at large, they are fully prepared to turn their faces southward to seek the means where they may establish for themselves and their posterity the system of employment by which they will be able to exclude themselves from poverty by inculcating the habits of industry and soberness. In the field of husbandry proscription will cease to harrass those through whose labor the development of the resources of the soil will depend, and open to them the avenues for social improvement in all the departments where the colored man will be measured in the circle of social elevation according to the standard of the mind by which the intelligent community will be governed.

The Basis of the Union between the Two Races.

Having exhausted the general principles that underlie the leading features of the several subjects that involves the destiny of the colored people in this country, let the proposition emanating from them be submitted to the statesmen and the philanthropists that they may examine the basis upon which the happiness of the two races may be *fully established under the guidance of the Unseen Hand that controls the existence of nations and the human family without any aid.*

The following will be considered as the protocol, with the points to indicate with some clearness the subject they will be called upon to give their support in behalf of posterity and the welfare of the nation.

1st. Let the appeal be made to every planter in the non-reconstructed States to grant alotments of not more than ten (10) acres to constitute a homestead for every family on the plantations where they were formerly held, and the same, with the right in fee, when acquired as herein provided, will exist in the family and their posterity forever, and will be exempt from all the disabilities, of every nature, by which the title of the lands could in any way be alienated under any process resulting from the decision of any court of law, or otherwise.

2d. As the object is to restore the relations of the freedmen to the soil as the agricultural class, and establish them in the position that will be permanent, and with the means to be useful among the planters, it is essential that they should labor for those who may extend the concession that will give to every family on any plantation a freehold interest in the land they may occupy, therefore let them render service under a mutual contract, in lieu of cash payment for the purchase.

The guardian of the nation as assumed over this people, imposes upon it the responsibility of making the necessary provisions to surrender it to the keeping of the States respectively, that their protection may become the duty of citizens at large to each other. For nothing would tend to demoralize the two races to a greater degree, than to throw them into a sudden contact without any fixed principles to govern them in cases where the struggle for the supremacy would form any part of the antagonism that would exist from the want of the regulations that should clearly point out the fraternal duty imposed upon them by the new relation in which they will stand to each other.

3d. To infuse into the agricultural interest in the Southern States the necessary vigor, and enable the people to re-establish their prosperity within the limits of the time they were engaged in destroying it, and reach a higher position than they could possibly attain by the ordinary means of recuperation, it is proper to extend to those who may have the disposition to rise above their present condition, such relief from the national treasury as may be necessary to enable such persons to cultivate the land, and give employment to the freedmen as occupants of grants made to them by virtue of the obligation that will be assumed in every case where the aid is extended.

Viewing it as the imperative duty of the people of the loyal States to take up the subject with sufficient vigor to show its economy when considered from the national standpoint from which it will be seen by the statesmen who feel the gravity of the proposition to supply homes for 4,000,000 of persons made free by virtue of the actions of the Federal Government, it is essential that the demand should be made upon the nation for 50,000,000 of dollars to carry out the plan of restoration and recuperation. It contemplates no discrimination on account of the political proclivities of any who may make the demand for relief, as the object is to seek the same liberality for the Freedmen on the plantations, who, from the relations they will sustain as citizens, and as cultivators of the soil, shall be free to follow their convictions without offending any one in the community.

4th. The organization of a Bureau of Agriculture in each of the several States by the legislatures, will give the people control of the measures by which homesteads should be arranged on the plantations where the owners will make the concession a voluntary act, with the co-operation of the Commissioners of Freedmen who would represent the Government of the United States in the performance of the duty that would be required to restore these people and secure certificates of title for every homestead and register the same in the county where located, which will constitute a deed of conveyance for all time to come. The purpose is to secure by legislation the exemption for the planters, and protect them to the extent required for the freedmen and keep them and their descendants together, and thereby afford the opportunity to trace the sublimity of the transition and the union between the two races for the generations to come, who will see in the spectacle the glorious results of the efforts to unite them through the industry of the country, and realize in the United States in a higher degree the blessings that were sought for by Solon in behalf of the Athenians.

To perpetuate the happiness of the people of the agricultural districts as far as human laws can promote it, it should not be lawful to issue any writ of attachment, excepting against the product of the plantations, and only so far as it may affect the planter in his special interest, and thereby protect the lien of the freedmen from the knavery that could be practiced upon them. If the loan is extended and judiciously employed in the improvement and in the cultivation of the land, with the use of the same for five years without any interest, it would give all the support that could be required for the accomplishment of the grand object contemplated by the demand upon the nation for that purpose.

In the purchase of lands for the freedmen the limit for payment should be extended to five years without any interest, which will enable them to relieve themselves of all incumbrances by the expiration of the time to refund the national loan, which will leave the two people in the condition to promote their prosperity and secure a lasting inheritance for their posterity, through the magnanimity by which the Federal Government will be prompted to come to the rescue.

5th. Brings the people of the United States to the consideration of another grave subject, and in which the claims of the widows and the orphans in the Southern States, upon whom the weight of the war has fallen with an irresistable force, and leaving them far beyond the reach of any succour from the source from which it should come for their relief. It has been shown, how necessary it will be to the peace of the country to ignore the political proclivity of the people in the agricultural field, and what may be demanded in this case in compliance with the exigency of the nation will be fully sustained where the claims of humanity will justify it in another in behalf of the class of sufferers for whose benefit the national loan could be applied as a donation when collected through the Bureau of Agriculture in the several States. When their condition is considered as it was before the war and compare it with their present situation, it seems to be the severest calamity that could possibly overtake the widows and the orphans, while the State through which they are suffering is powerless and can afford them no relief. The law of humanity that justifies the succour extended to the wounded enemy upon the field of slaughter, points with more force to the duty of the community to build up institutions for the protection and the education of the fatherless children. But there is another phase that must be reached to make the subject as comprehensive as possible, for while the nation may never be in the situation to extend its pension roll to the Southern States, as those who would seek its benefits were employed against the Federal Government, yet as it is impossible to leave the decrepid in the misery entailed upon them by the incidents of the struggle, therefore the duty of the people of the several States ought to be very clear in reference to all of that class and especially where they have no resources to fall back upon. But *what would stand in the way of the legislatures making the necessary provision for them if the gravity of the subject should have sufficient weight to bring out the approval of the Government and the people of the loyal States*, is the question that will come up for consideration. If it is universally conceded that without secession there would have been no emancipation in the Southern States, then it will be seen in the general result how far the good will preponderate against the evil of the mission it has performed for the nation; therefore let the entire country submit to the contingencies and heal up the breach that all may rejoice together.

To employ the fifty millions of dollars, ($50,000,000) in establishing homes for the invalids and in building up other institutions for the widows and orphans, would give it a two-fold character and make the benefits ramify through every circle of society in that section of the country, and when the sacrifice the amount in green-

backs would cost the United States in materials and in the manu-
factory is carefully considered, it seems to be impossible for the
proposition to fail without carrying with it the dignity of the
Republic.

As the last point of the protocol has been considered, it will now
afford the opportunity to take a retrospective view of the subject to
enable the people of this country to comprehend more fully the
nature and the magnitude of the plan, and the efforts of the colored
man to supply the means to arrive at the solution of the questions
by peaceful means, that have cost the nation the vast sacrifice of
blood and treasure, while it presents not a single feature that could
not be reached without it. It is decidedly more pleasant to enter
upon this field of labor, for it is here where the evidence at hand
will give the necessary force to the subject, and carry it above the
criticism to which it may at any time have been exposed from the
want of information in reference to the secret purpose of the plan
submitted to many of the leading statesmen who were called upon
to review it.

But it is worthy of note, that no party in this country could
have adopted the plan without entering into the revolutionary
policy it aimed to infuse, by making the emancipation of all the
females in the several States, by compensation, the leading feature,
and by the development of the utility of free labor elsewhere than
in the Territories, and neutralize the theory of the class of public
men who were "the representatives of white men," and consequently
ignored the interest of the colored people entirely.

But as they have been driven from the position by the development of the principles which makes them the representatives of
the American people, it will afford them the means to study and
learn something from the fallacy which neutralized their usefulness
and carried the country to the verge of disruption.

The vigor with which the pen of colored men may be employed,
in compliance with the duty imposed upon them by their elevation
in the scale of manhood, will preclude the necessity for any apology
for the course that will be pursued, without any reference to the
views of others, to fix the destiny of the race among the people of
the United States.

THE DANGER OF SECESSION CONSIDERED IN THE APPEAL TO THE
PEOPLE OF SOUTH CAROLINA IN BEHALF OF THE UNION.

Having carefully considered the tendency and the danger of
secession in advance of the developments that led to its inaugura-
tion, the copy of the document, as preserved, will show the correct-
ness of the premises and will give those whom it was designed to
serve, a better opportunity to study the colored people than they
will ever learn of them from the stand-point from which they
were seen by the statesmen of the country.

" BEDFORD, L. I. October 31, 1860.

" To his Excellency GOVERNOR GIST.

"SIR: Hoping that your excellency will carefully consider the
subject of this letter and weigh its contents for the benefit of the
people of South Carolina, I deem it important to submit it to you.
It is the first of the series of documents that will be submitted to
the Governors, and to the Legislatures of the several States, to un-
fold the principles by which the nation may be governed to escape
the danger to which it is exposed, from the cause of the commotion
in the public mind. The distance which the Statesmen of the
Southern and Northern States have been led from each other, will
preclude them from originating any plan to control the country
upon principles that would command the approval of the people in
both sections with the means they have employed for that purpose.
If this point is well taken, the necessity for a remedy to relieve
the people from the suspense created by the intensity of the excite-
ment in the public mind, will be admitted by your Excellency, and
if I should succeed in establishing the position of the arbitrator to
settle the sectional contest on the question of slavery and emancipation, it will enable me to command the attention of those to whom
I will make the appeal in behalf of my own people.

"My complexion as a colored man, will be a guarantee for the
sincerity of my intention, and the efforts I have made to serve
the people of the Southern States, with the plan to relieve them

from the danger of the policy by which they are governed; and if continued in it can lead to no other result than the overthrow of the very principle it is intended to protect. To deal with this subject intelligently, two things must be considered by your Excellency and the honorable members of the legislature of South Carolina, upon whom it will devolve to fix the principles by which the people of that State will be governed in the future, in reference to the subject of emancipation as a southern measure with a national basis.

"The mathematical considerations that must be gone into to comprehend every phase the subject will undergo, whether it assume an extreme Southern aspect in all its ramifications or developments, be made to make it harmonize with the interests of the country without any injustice to the people in either section. That this attempt on my part may be useful to the efforts to preserve the peace of the country, the position and the intention of the people of the Southern States at the present time must be considered in connection with the principles by which they were governed at the formation of the government, and if it can be seen that there is a departure from the line of policy established by the delegates in the convention in 1787, the extenuating cause must be reviewed without any disguise.

"If it is admitted that the African slave trade continued twenty years in compliance with the demand of the delegates from Georgia and South Carolina, and that the time fixed upon for its termination was sanctioned by them, then it is very important to know whether the people of these two States will stand by the compact to protect the dignity of the nation or whether they will abandon it without any regard to it! This is the question that must be answered in harmony with the views of the people who are opposed to the slave trade, or it must assume an aspect that will accord with the disposition to favor it regardless of the consequences which may follow. The gravity of the subject will be fully developed if considered in connection with the progress of public opinion in the free States which is sweeping before it every effort that tends to favor the slave trade as an issue before the people of this country. If the convention surrendered to it in 1787, the position the Southern States will assume at this crisis will show the magnanimity and the loyalty of the people to the Union.

"The fact that the legislature of South Carolina will be called upon to deal with this subject with a view to abandon the ultra Southern policy by which her statesmen have been controlled, is of the highest importance, as the safety of that section of the country depends upon the wisdom and the forbearance of the people who must sacrifice principles which cannot be sustained without exposing them to an extremity that may lead to the gravest consequences. The necessity for guarding against creating any suspicion in the mind of Southern men, led me to suppress the subject of my mission until the exigencies of the times would enable me to make the effort to submit it to the legislatures of the several States with the approval of the people of this country. The impression that I could make it useful to the nation and promote the interest of my own people, was too deeply fixed in my mind to permit me to look with indifference upon the efforts of the statesmen in the development of principles against the peace of the country and its internal relations, if not revolutionary in their tendency, without carrying with them any benefit to the colored people.

"That your Excellency and the honorable members of the legislature may fully comprehend the magnitude and the gravity of the subject and the necessity of submitting it at this juncture, I will reveal the policy I have followed in my appeals to the legislatures of some of the Southern States to make agriculture the basis of emigration to Africa. If it was the intention to remove the free colored people from motives of philanthropy, the elaborate plan devised for that purpose by me is sufficient to carry it out to the fullest extent without exposing them to the penalty of confiscating the freedom of any. But if the object was the re-enslavement of my people I considered it my duty to stand between them and the State Legislatures as far as I could to shield them against any legislation without the real object being fully revealed. Three appeals were made to the legislature of Virginia during the last two administrations, two of which were very important to the free colored people of that State, as the question was pending each time to enact a law to enslave them if they did not leave within time limited for that purpose. In each case the proposition failed and the prompting of humanity was triumphant in the Legislature, which is the only refuge for that proscribed people. Appeals were

made to Maryland, Tennessee, Indiana, Georgia and Florida, and
without expecting or having received any reply, yet the result of
my efforts to save the colored people with the plan of emigration
were fully established by the proceedings of the legislatures where
it was considered. The necessity of adopting it as a policy by
which the people of the Southern States could lead the country
was elaborately gone into, not only in the documents to the Legislatures but in the letters written to influential men in that section
of the Union. The fact that the South has lost the opportunity and
is thrown back upon the people of the free States, upon whom it
will depend to make the plan of emigration the limits to the efforts
in behalf of the colored people until emancipation can be mutually
considered, is the phase the subject must assume. The two-fold
object I had in view having been developed as far as possible, it
was not necessary that I should lose any time with intelligent men
who stood in a position to avail themselves of the useful aspect of
the subject or ignore it if they had no disposition to apply it as the
solution to the question for the elevation of the free colored people.
The scale upon which it was submitted to the legislatures of New
York and New Jersey will enable me to establish the non-sectional
position upon which the claims of the race may be submitted to
the country. The aspect it will assume in the free States will be
very important, inasmuch as the philanthropy of the American
people will lead to its adoption to save the colored people or it will
prove itself insufficient for that object from the want of sincerity.
If your Excellency will examine the subject it will be seen that the
support of the people of the Southern States will give it the necessary force and make it precede any attempt to reach the question
of emancipation which must be considered in connection with the
demand for laborers in the South. If the modification of the laws
of the several States can be carried with a view to make up the
deficit with free labor, it would afford the necessary relief with far
less danger than it would to seek it by opening the slave trade.
Sooner or later this subject will develop itself to the States of the
South and will be seen as a necessity that must be met for the relief
of the people. To admit free labor in the Southern States whether
colored or white, would not only be important to the planters, but
it would be equally important to the colored people in the free
States, who must seek a refuge somewhere.

"As desirous as I am for the emancipation and the elevation of my people, and believing that the dissolution of the Union would preclude the necessity of any legislation upon the subject, yet as I consider it a duty to humanity to urge a policy that will protect the innocent and lead to mutual efforts by the people of the United States to accomplish that object, I will submit it and trust to their wisdom for success. It would be a fatal mistake to suppose that the future of the colored people in this country can be known from their past history, for in spite of the degrading position they occupy they would not fail to seize up on any opportunity that would enable them to prove their devotion to the cause of Freedom. The fact that the Union with the means to develop the resources, would be far more advantageous to the Southern States than could possibly be derived out of it, is a grave subject and cannot be ignored under any contingency that may occur, if the welfare of the people should govern the statesmen. Without reviewing the difficulties that would arise from the necessity of a foreign policy, I will leave the subject, believing that the people will not be driven from their loyalty by mere apprehension. By a reference to the speech made at "Sleepy Hollow" by a distinguished Senator in South Carolina some two years since, the statement was made to the effect, "That the sympathy for" the free colored people "in the free States is not sufficient to cause any apprehension to the South." That is true, and while that address was condemned and repudiated in the South, yet its safety depends upon the policy embodied in it. For while the Senate and the House of Representatives, and the Executive of the United States will at no distant day be under the control of those who will be opposed to the slave trade, and to the extension of slavery, and will aim to place the government where it stood at the commencement of its existence, yet from the very nature of things, it will be harmless to the South. If the purity of the government is necessary to its existence to secure it by removing the cause of legislative conspiracy to sustain sectional issues, is an object that will commend itself to every considerate statesman of the country. In connection with this letter, I will send a copy of my pamphlet which contains the text of the subject in all its ramifications, and I will supply copies for the members of the legislature as soon as I can. It is not my intention to submit to the legislature the plan of emigration to create a neutral position upon this subject which may be very important to the people, until the new order of things are fully developed in favor of emancipation.

"Hoping that this will be considered as an object worthy of the attention of your Excellency and the people, it is respectfully submitted by your obedient servant."

"L. H. PUTNAM."

———

Looking to the objects to be obtained from the success of this as a national work, will preclude the necessity of seeking from any higher source the right to speak as by authority, and taking as the text, the subject by which the way to the legislature of South Carolina was fully prepared previous to the war. For as the sequel has brought with it all the consequences referred to in the appeal submitted as a warning by one of that proscribed class, it is important to confront the people at the point where the first shock to the Union was felt, that the remedy for the calamity that has fallen with equal force upon the other States of the rebellion may be applied.

For what they failed to learn with the aid of their superior intelligence in the first place, they will fully comprehend from the reflex of the *light which the minds of black men may emit in the struggle to maintain the ideas promulgated by the framers of the Declaration of Independence.*

The first point of any importance that will present itself to the reflecting mind, will be seen in the want of appreciation and in the condemnation of the speech made at "Sleepy Hollow" by an ardent supporter of State sovereignty, and which will go very far to fix the impression that nothing but the stern results that have followed the catastrophe of the battle-field, could in the slightest degree arrest . the designs of those who were guiding the destiny of the south without any reference to the power, and the higher laws that governs the universe.

For it was too true, as stated by the distinguished Senator of
South Carolina, that there was nothing to show that any *sympathy
existed for the colored people in the free States, sufficient to alarm
the South,* and it was from a similar conviction created in the mind
of the writer of the document that prompted him to take part in the
efforts to arrive at a solution of the questions by which the country
was agitated, and aiming at results directly opposite to the policy
by which public men were governed.

The second point is the value of the document as an indication
of the disposition to shield from danger those who were aiming to
perpetuate the oppression of the colored people, and the secret history and the magnitude of the work written for that purpose will
fix for all time to come its grandeur and the design to guide the
efforts for emancipation and elevation in this country.

But while the developments that will be made upon this subject
will be more than sufficient to indicate the inflexible devotion of the
author to the cause of universal liberty, yet it is proper that some
reference should be made in this connection to other branches of
the subject extending to the Russian Empire, and to Dahomey in
Africa, and will form part of the great work that must be performed
for the benefit of the human family.

The first is the efforts to devise a plan to fix the relations of the
emancipated in Russia to the soil, and to show the fact that it was
accomplished at the time when it could not fail to be useful, as an
object that would merit some attention in that country. The means
employed to have the plan submitted to the Emperor, would have
been ample in either of the two channels fixed upon for the purpose, as
the civility of the Baron, as a member of the Legation at Washington, was only equal to the attention given to the subject by the American Minister previous to his return to St. Petersburgh.

At the interview with the latter at the St. Nicholas Hotel in
the City of New York, a full exposition was made to show the feasi-
bility of elevating the emancipated above the condition of tenants
at will, which is slavery in the second degree, by securing for every
family the right in fee to homesteads on the estates of the nobles.

The reference that may be made to the plan as an agency to emancipation in the Brazillian Empire, and also in the Colonies of Spain, seems to be sufficient in its magnitude to make a serious impression in the minds of the people, and upon the two governments, from the necessity by which they will be led by the force of circumstances, sooner or later to maintain the relations of the emancipated with the soil by a freehold interest the same as will be demanded by the agricultural interests in the Southern States. To those who are in need of information, let them seek it in the result of the transition of twenty millions, (20,000,000) of persons in the Russian Empire, from the condition of serfs to the elevation of freemen. But while the plan was not published as contemplated, yet the adoption of the principles by the command of the Emperor will afford all the consolation that could be derived from the effect of the measures that will lead to a complete revolution in the social relations of the peasantry of that country as the agricultural class, and upon the unborn millions who will enjoy the blessings it will confer upon them.

The communication written to the Minister of Foreign Affairs for the purpose of submitting to the government of her Majesty the Queen of England, the plan for the suppression of the slave trade, and the annual custom of the King of Dahomey, with an elaborate exposition of the views, and indicating the means by which the entire people could be led to conform to the principles of civilization, and at the same time avoid the system of absorption that would tend to make the country an English Colony, will fully repay for the labor it cost.

The declaration made in the British Parliament by Lord John Russell the Minister of Foreign Affairs, to the effect, that the influence of England was ample to control the King, opened the way for the attempt to show the necessity of employing it in behalf of civilization in the section of the continent of Africa, which was known to be the great mart of the slave trade.

In looking at the subject of the labor to promote the happiness of mankind, let us pause here and contemplate upon the grandeur and the effect of the change upon the social condition of society from the adoption of the homestead system in other countries, where hostility against color is not carried to the extent to which it prevails in the United States, and where a large portion of those who are friends of freedom have yet to reach the point to enable them to favor the elevation of the Freedmen with the aim to break up caste.

But the extraordinary rapidity with which the country is driven will be sufficient to change the spirit of the people and enable them to see in the colored man an ally on whom they must depend. To confound those in their schemes against freedom, and neutralize their designs would indeed be an object of the highest importance, but to accomplish it, it will depend upon the ability of colored men to suggest measures that will merit the approval of all who are disposed to recognize the power they must exercise to rise to any position of distinction in the Republic. For if it is possible to make the commencement at any time, let us try to do it from this point, by throwing out the planks for the construction of a national platform in the Southern States, and cover the ground others would occupy, to the injury of our race if they had the materials at hand.

The first object to be accomplished by the development of the principles embodied in this work, is to make it the precursor of the elements by which the colored people will be carried to the elevation that will be made for them by the surrender of the pretension to superiority that cannot be sustained by other means than the assumption by which the dominant class have been governed in this country. Therefore it is the duty of the leading men to enter the field, not as advocates of any exclusive class, but to demonstrate their abilities to deal with the questions of the day with dignity and intelligence and thereby command the attention and the respect of public opinion. While the labor will fall on the few who are educated up to the times, yet under the guidance of Providence, they must make themselves equal to the requirements of the untutored mass who are exposed to the criticism of those who will struggle to the last to resist the current of the revolution by which the nation is carried onward in its new mission.

Programme is :

1. The enlargement of the work by adding to it documents and important letters to leading statesmen in the Southern and Northern States.

2. The issue of the second number of the pamphlet for distribution, with the history of the mission from its origin, with the necessary reference to those who inspired the author with the ideas that led him to assume it, and enable them to learn that all the attempts to " withdraw" from it, have increased the vigor by which they were held as the repository of the plan of the revolution in behalf of Freedom, and of the reputation of the man who had no other dependence as the shield excepting in the merits of the work, for his elevation in the public mind.

3. The labor in the Southern States with the design to reach the people at large, without any reference to their views on the topic of the day, and infuse the spirit of the work in the minds of the colored people that they may comprehend the purpose of the union between capital and labor, and perform as freemen the duty of citizens of the Republic.

APPENDIX.

The intention is to revise and enlarge the review by adding to it a document on the financial policy of the nation as a criticism on the subject of specie payment. The want of a comprehensive plan for the management of the question cannot fail to create the impression that it has completely overwhelmed the ideas of those who are struggling to reach a solution that will settle the basis for the currency of the country. This is a grave subject, inasmuch as it involves the integrity of the government of the United States through the measures of the statesmen who must show that they are equal to the requirements as managers.

They are bound to bring to an end the policy by which gold and silver were transformed from a currency into a commodity for speculation, with the Treasury Department as the centre. It must be shown that the exigency that forced the greenbacks into use has ceased and the system fixed upon for the withdrawal of these promises and if not, then a fiscal agency should be established to sustain it upon a specie basis.

While the theory of the Ohio statesman in favor of the extension of the issue of this circulating medium is sustained by the views advanced in the same direction by the members of the House from Massachusetts and other leading minds of the country, and is not without its plausible features, and yet the fatal mistake they have made by not making a distinction between the provisional use of the greenbacks and the want of a permanent system by which the nation may separate its financial management from the commercial interest as involved in its connection with the National Banks, by the organization of the necessary fiscal agency to sustain it, therefore, they must fail.

The innocency and the earnestness with which the subject has been submitted to the public seems to be wholly inadequate for the display of the brilliant ideas that should emanate from the minds of men of genius, inasmuch as the aim is to issue an amount of greenbacks far greater than it would be in the power of the government to control with any degree of honesty.

The next object of the enlargement will be for the production of letters that were written to prominent men with the view to bring out some action in behalf of the plan to promote free labor in the Southern States in connection with the efforts to make emigration a national question. The labor expended to make the subject worthy of the attention of the managers of the colonization society and to carry it out through its agency will of itself present a record that will be as grand as it will be important to the public and to the class of friends who gave it their support. Organized as that institution was to represent the philanthropy of the nation in behalf of the colored people and under the control of some of the ablest minds of the country, and having assumed the position as a promoter of the cause, it is necessary that my relation with it should become the subject of criticism by the public. It will be seen that the danger of the absorption of the society by the operation of the plan to make agriculture the basis of emigration, and the inroad upon the policy by which it was governed from its existence was fully developed upon a scale that completely neutralized the design of those who had given it their sanction and support. The cause of the hardship suffered by the emigrants seems to have been a subject of very little moment to the managers, or else the necessity for relief was concealed from them by the reports made from time to time in reference to the real condition of things in Liberia.

The proposition to establish a farm in that country to cultivate coffee, cotton, rice and indigo to demonstrate the necessity of an entire change in their plan of emigration was carried into operation with their knowledge by sending ·out a person with a full supply of agricultural implements with ample provision for his support. To make it the personal property of myself and associate I propose to establish one hundred ten acre farms for as many families (free from any charge to them) out of the annual product under the direction or supervision of the board of managers. But the want of a comprehensive idea of the magnitude of the plan and its purpose at the outset was their misfortune, and the means resorted to to withdraw this influence as the remedy, was not only against their genius but it was a betrayal of the weakness in the management of the colonization society. The importance of this discovery, in connection with the result of the examination carefully made, into the commercial operations carried on with Liberia, was fully considered and the means adopted to make it known to the public. It was the commencement of the work to dig under its foundation, and prepare the way for the absorption of the entire organization by the efforts to establish a board of five Commissioners in every State, under the supervision of the legislatures with the Governors as *ex-officio* members, to sustain emigration to Africa with the support of Congress. This was the plan to establish thirty-one districts through the agency of the government of Liberia, to represent for six hundred families in each of the several States, and to cost six million dollars ($6,000,000).

The plan was not only submitted to the managers of the New York State Colonization Society, and was the subject of debate during an entire sitting; but it was transmitted to the annual meeting of the board of directors of the American Colonization Society in Washington, with an elaborate exposition of the commercial policy. These documents in effect were regular bomb-shells, and especially to the new delegation, and was the occasion of the most exciting session ever held by that body. As the adoption of the plan would have been the end of the New York board of managers, the cause of its resistance will be worthy of the most serious attention. The most important result was the abandonment of the commercial operation, as it was carried on in the name of the Colonization Society, which shows the disposition of the Board to shield its honor, and the reputation of its members against the doings of its agents.

This reference to the secret history is to show that the society in this State was "*driven on by the law of self-preservation to struggle for its existence.*" It enables me to assume the position to defy the members of the Board of Managers individually and collectively, to make the attempt to occupy any other ground than that. Fortified as I am behind the three hundred pages of documents with twelve circulars hid away in the archives of the Board of Managers and of the Board of Directors of the American Colonization Society it is the point to which they must look.

The confidence reposed in me by friends of my race, and the progress and the blessings bestowed upon me, good men were duly cherished, and by which I was sustained in the darkest hours of the struggle to overcome all opposition and stand before the country as a worthy representative of the colored people, and an honorable citizen of the Republic.

www.ingramcontent.com/pod-product-compliance
Lightning Source LLC
Chambersburg PA
CBHW021440090426
42739CB00009B/1564